get up, please

get up, please

POEMS ✣ DAVID KIRBY

Louisiana State University Press
Baton Rouge

Published by Louisiana State University Press
Copyright © 2016 by David Kirby
All rights reserved
Manufactured in the United States of America
FIRST PRINTING

Designer: Barbara Neely Bourgoyne
Typefaces: Requiem and Gotham, display; Adobe Caslon Pro, text
Printer and binder: Cushing-Malloy, Inc.

Many thanks to the editors of the following journals, where versions of these poems first appeared: *American Poetry Review:* "You've Built Your Own Mosque"; *Ampersand:* "Oh, Well"; *Cincinnati Review:* "Is Spot in Heaven?"; *Five Points:* "The Juniper Tree"; *Gettysburg Review:* "Ode to Disappointment"; *Gulf Coast:* "If I Don't Go Crazy"; *Kenyon Review:* "The Juggler of Notre-Dame"; *Memorious:* "John Keats"; *Oxford American:* "Taking It Home to Jerome"; *Pleiades:* "I Believe You Are Death"; *Poetry London:* "The Minotaur"; *Smartish Pace:* "Girl Groups"; *Southern Review:* "All My Jellies," "Mrs. Jones," "The Nematode," and "Old Poets"; *Spillway:* "Let's Take Off"; *Superstition Review:* "Come to Find Out" and "A Few Old Things"; *Terminus:* "Gnürszk" and "John the Conqueror"; *Upstreet:* "Ode to Lists." "Get Up, Please" appeared on the Academy of American Poetry's Poem-a-Day site. "Is Spot in Heaven?" appeared in *Best American Poetry 2015.*

LIBRARY OF CONGRESS CATALOGING-IN-PUBLICATION DATA

Kirby, David, 1944–
[Poems. Selections]
Get up, please : poems / David Kirby.
pages ; cm
ISBN 978-0-8071-6290-3 (hardcover : acid-free paper) — ISBN 978-0-8071-6289-7 (softcover : acid-free paper) — ISBN 978-0-8071-6291-0 (pdf) — ISBN 978-0-8071-6292-7 (epub) — ISBN 978-0-8071-6293-4 (mobi)
I. Title.
PS3561.I66A6 2016
811'.54—dc23

2015033302

CONTENTS

get up, please

IF I DON'T GO CRAZY

There's a sheriff's car parked near Emerald Mound,
and the deputy is looking down at his lap and smiling,
        which means he's probably doing what everyone else is doing
these days, that is, texting, though I think he's knitting a quilt
        out of the scalps he's taken off travelers like me:

        a killer has been working these country roads of late
with a blue flashing light, pulling people over and shooting
        them for fun, like the men who lived in caves on the Natchez
Trace in the day and who killed travelers for money and then
        because they found out how much they liked killing.

        I wonder if those men might not have been okay if they'd
just had girlfriends. What are the blues? A man losing
        his woman, some say, or the other way around. If I don't
go crazy, says Son House, I'm going to lose my mind.
        Damned straight: you're working twelve-hour days

        at the Dockery or Stovall Plantation and can barely get up most
mornings and owe more than you earn, but you can play
        and sing a little, and there's this gal who looks at you from time
to time, and her name is Louise McGhee, and you tell her
        you're playing at the Honeydipper this Saturday and ask

        if she'd like to come hear you, and she smiles and says yes,
yes, I would, and on the night of the show, you wait for the other
        fellows to finish and you get up there and say How's everybody
doing tonight and you look out into the crowd, and sure
        enough, there's Louise, your pearl beyond price, your last

chance at happiness in a world where a man works like
an animal till the day he dies and lands in jail if he drinks
        too much or looks at the wrong person the wrong way,
but she's with another fellow, and it's like she can't keep
                her hands off him, and you grin and you sing, but inside

                you're thinking, God damn every goddamned thing to hell,
and when you finish, there's some coins in your tip jar
        and even a dollar bill or two, and a couple of fellows pull
their pints out, and you take a few sips, long ones,
                but on your way home, when you know nobody's watching,

                you grab your guitar like a baseball bat and swing it
against a tree. How do you write the song that gets the girl?
        If we knew the answer to that one, we'd all have somebody.
Ma Rainey is a vaudeville singer in 1902 when she hears
                a young miss in a little town sing what she later describes

                as a "strange and poignant lament" about a bad man,
so Ma starts doing the song herself, and suddenly America
        hears the blues. A year later, W. C. Handy is cooling his heels
late one night in the Tutwiler, Mississippi train station when,
                in his words, he dozes and wakes to the sounds of a "lean,

                loose-jointed Negro" pressing a knife blade to his guitar
strings and playing "the weirdest music I had ever heard."
        Mr. Handy doesn't know whether he's dreaming this
or not: "Going where the Southern cross the Dog,"
                says the singer, that is, where the Southern Line intersects

the Yazoo & Mississippi, the crossroad, which is where,
finally, you have a choice, because you thought you were
        going one place in your life and now you see you can go
left or right or even back home, if you want, but no,
        you want to go someplace new, someplace you haven't

        been before, even if it's way the hell out in the country,
out there by the cemetery, the one so old they don't even
        bury folks in it these days, and the wind's picking up,
and a man steps over a fallen headstone, a big man,
        and he has something in his hands, and you don't know

        if it's a rifle or an axe, something he could hurt or even kill
you with, and you can't see his face, but he holds out this thing
        he's carrying, and it's a guitar, and he says, "Here,
I tuned this for you, take it," and you know if you do, you'll be lost,
        but you'll do anything to get that woman back,

        anything at all, so you rest that guitar on your knee
and you run your thumb down the strings, and a thousand birds
        cry at once, and the smell of lavender rises from
the hard ground at your feet, and you think you see a line
        of people against the sky's last light but you can't tell

        where they're going, and you glance at the trees, and their
branches are thick with slave ships and Spanish galleons,
        and you say "Who the hell are you?" and the man shakes
his head and points, and his mouth doesn't move,
        and a voice you never want to hear again says, "Play."

JOHN KEATS

Fanny Brawne chides him because he loves her
for her beauty. "Why may I not speak of your Beauty,"
    says John Keats, "since without that I could never have
lov'd you? I cannot conceive any beginning of such love
        as I have for you but Beauty." See, she thinks he means

        the way she looks, and, sure, most men start with
a handsome bosom or a well-turned ankle, but after that,
    men love women the way women love men, so that "beauty"
doesn't mean "looks" but something like "the whole
        package." Did not John Keats describe her to

        his brother George as "beautiful and elegant, graceful,
silly, fashionable and strange"? Who would not want
    to be thought "silly" and "strange" by John Keats!
Of his own looks, John Keats writes, "I am not a thing
        to be admired. . . . I hold that place among Men which

        snub-nos'd brunettes with meeting eyebrows do among
women—they are trash to me—unless I should find one
    among them with a fire in her heart like the one that burns
in mine." On the one hand, I think John Keats
        is just fishing for compliments, the way we all do when

        we say, "Oh, this old rag? It's the only clean thing
I could find" or "It's kind of you to say that about
    my poem/story/screenplay, but it still needs a lot of work."
On the other, the fire that burned in John Keats's heart
        is like one of those 8,000-acre wildfires you see on TV,

the ones that burn everything in their paths yet leave
the earth ready for fresh growth—woe to the lover
      who cannot match the heat of that inferno! "In case
of the worst that can happen, I shall still love you,"
            says John Keats, "but what hatred shall I have for another!"

            Oh, don't say that, John Keats! Jealousy's the meanest
emotion. Terror, anger, sorrow, joy: these burn the way
      that fire in your heart does, blue and pure, whereas jealousy
smokes and sputters and makes you look noisome and puny.
            Better to ask Fanny for a letter from her own hand,

            to say "write the softest words and kiss them that I may
at least touch my lips where yours have been," and, then,
      when you get it, "I have kiss'd your Writing
over in the hope you had indulg'd me by leaving a trace
            of honey." Of course: if you're going to die, why not

            do it with Fanny Brawne's lips on yours? Or John Keats's.
His friend Severn says his last words were "lift me up—
      I am dying—I shall die easy; don't be frightened—be firm,
and thank God it has come." Fine, though just two months
            earlier, he's saying this about Fanny to Charles Brown:

            "I can bear to die—I cannot bear to leave her. Oh, God!
God! God! Every thing I have in my trunks that reminds
      me of her goes through me like a spear." Oh, God!
God! God! There's nothing sweeter than the right word
            to the right person at the right time, nothing sadder, nothing

more likely to buoy you up like the scape of a dandelion
floating toward heaven, to drag you down to a hell
        hotter than the hottest hell you've ever imagined.
Don't just sit there, reader. Do something! There's a wildfire
            headed your way. Throw water on it—no, wait, gasoline.

THE JUNIPER TREE

Bill hands me a book called *Dr. Mary's Monkey,* and it's not
                very well written, but how can you resist
        the story of an unsolved murder, a secret laboratory, Lee
Harvey Oswald, the JFK assassination, cancer-causing monkey viruses,
                and the outbreak of global epidemics
        that, if the book is everything it claims to be, are just around

the corner, and as I'm turning the pages and thinking,
                That's not true, and that's probably not true, and that might
        be true but it certainly isn't described very well, I realize
that the Dr. Mary in the book is *my* Dr. Mary, that is,
                the Dr. Mary Sherman who treated me for polio when
        I was a little boy, scared that I wouldn't be able to run

around outside the way the other boys did, wouldn't be able
                to do sports like other boys and attract girls and eventually
        find my own Dr. Mary, who was, well, "stacked," built like
Jane Russell, say, though older than Jane, yet who shone
                on me with a warmth more incandescent than that
        of ten Jane Russells. And then she died horribly, but I always

thought I'd get Dr. Mary back. As I lay in bed and waited
                for my legs to heal, sometimes at night my father would lie
        down beside me and read from a book of fairy tales,
and the one I always wanted to hear was the story called
                "The Juniper Tree," in which a man and his wife
        want a child desperately, but she dies in childbirth, and his second

wife hates the boy and loves only her own daughter,
                and one day she slams the lid of a chest on him and knocks
        his head off. When my children were tiny, I used to think,

What if something terrible happens to them? And then
                I'd think, What if it doesn't? Usually it doesn't. In fairy
        tales, you're always rescued: you suffer, yeah, but you get

the prince or your children are returned to you or you live
                forever, if that's your idea of a rescue. I was ten when
        I was Dr. Mary's patient, and she was forty, and, if the book
is to be believed, was working in an underground medical
                lab to develop a biological weapon that would be used
        to kill Fidel Castro, where a witness also puts Oswald,

though the witness is Judyth Vary Baker, who would later
                write *Me & Lee: How I Came to Know, Love and Lose
        Lee Harvey Oswald.* Who could love Lee Harvey Oswald?
He always looks so sour in his photos. Good shot, though.
                Well, not really—he was a terrible marksman as a Marine,
        leading even smart people to say no, he couldn't have done it,

couldn't have hit a barn wall at ten paces, much less a moving
                U.S. president at 190 feet, must have been a patsy. For whom,
        though? CIA, Mafia, Cubans? The problem with the JFK
mystery is that those groups and a dozen others all had their
                guys in Dealey Plaza that day, not to mention most of
        the unaffiliated area nut jobs who just happened to be there

with their rifle, blowgun, crossbow, throwing knife,
                water pistol. After the bad mother in "The Juniper Tree"
        kills the little boy, she thinks, "Maybe I can get out of this"
and puts his head on his neck again and sits him in a chair
                and tricks her daughter, whose name is Marlene, into
        boxing his ears, and when she does and the boy's head

flies off, Marlene screams in terror as the mother tells her
                they can hide the crime by making a stew of his flesh,
         and when the father comes home, he wonders where
his beloved son is, true, but he's also hungry, so he eats
                the stew and even asks for more as Marlene stands
         by "crying and crying, and all her tears fell into the pot, and they

did not need any salt." In the Texas Book Depository, Oswald
                chambers a round in his mail-order rifle and squints
         through the scope. Pow, pow: one shot to the shoulder, another
to the head, and it's Johnny, we hardly knew ye. Less than
                a year later, Dr. Mary is found in her bed, her right arm
         and rib cage completely burned away, though the hair on

her head is untouched; investigators guess she was brought
                back to her apartment after suffering the burns somewhere
         else, such as, you got it, that secret lab where a malfunctioning
particle accelerator used to mutate monkey viruses sends out
                a high-voltage charge that hits Dr. Mary like a bolt
         of lightning. Dr. Mary—so warm, so vital, so encouraging to a sick

little boy, then found mutilated, half her body burned away,
                though her bedclothes were barely singed. Dark-eyed
         and pale, she looked like Snow White grown up. How can
she be dead? Night after night, my father reads me
                the same story, and night after night, Marlene buries
         her brother's bones beneath a juniper tree, and the juniper tree

begins to move, and a mist rises from it, and a fire appears
                in the mist, and a beautiful bird flies out of the fire
         and perches on the roof of the house and sings the most beautiful

song anyone has ever heard, and the father is happy
     again and says, "What a beautiful bird, and the sun
     is shining, and the air smells like cinnamon," and the bird gives

gives him a gold chain, and Marlene comes out, and the bird
     gives her red shoes, and the bad mother comes out,
     and the bird throws a millstone onto her head
and kills her, and smoke and flames pour out of the spot where she lies
     dead, and when they blow away, the little brother
     is standing there, alive as ever. Dr. Mary, I want to kiss your

beautiful face. I wanted to kiss you when I was a little boy,
     but I didn't know what kissing meant: I mean, grandmas,
     yeah, but not that kind. I'd be older than you are now,
so it'd be okay. Dr. Mary, you were my first crush.
     You were a pin-up to me but a saint as well, as beautiful
     as a martyr on an ancient wall. How I wish I could soften

the hearts of the gods and lead you out of the underworld,
     your fever cooled, your skin clear, your tongue ready
     to tell us all you know. Why do we kill one another?
Why do we love one another, and what is love? We say
     "I love you" to other people and they say "I love you, too"
     or "No, you don't"—how's that work? I see you as in

a swirl of smoke: I'm in a church like one in Rome, say,
     before a mosaic of gold and green and blue, and the wind
     is high outside, and the great door behind me blows open,
and when I turn to look, it slams shut, and the candles
     go out, or all but a few, and you step down from the wall,
     your eyes bright, your breath warm on my cheek,

and we walk out into the ancient city together,
          and I'm a little boy again, and I look up and say,
     "You saved me," and you say, "No, you saved me,"
and when you say it, suddenly I'm a man, taller than
          you are, and I take your hand in mine, and you say
you saved me, you saved me, all the way down to the river.

TAKING IT HOME TO JEROME

In Baton Rouge, there was a DJ on the soul station who was
always urging his listeners to "take it on home to Jerome."

No one knew who Jerome was. And nobody cared. So it
didn't matter. I was, what, ten, twelve? I didn't have anything

to take home to anyone. Parents and teachers told us that all
we needed to do in this world were three things: be happy,

do good, and find work that fulfills you. But I also wanted
to learn that trick where you grab your left ankle in your

right hand and then jump through with your other leg.
Everything else was to come, everything about love:

the sadness of it, knowing it can't last, that all lives must end,
all hearts are broken. Sometimes when I'm writing a poem,

I feel as though I'm operating that crusher that turns
a full-size car into a metal cube the size of a suitcase.

At other times, I'm just a secretary: the world has so much
to say, and I'm writing it down. This great tenderness.

ALL MY JELLIES

I'm riding shotgun as we tool around Memphis in Tad Pierson's
        '55 Cadillac, looking for the house where Johnny Cash lived
before he hit the big time, and people are shouting "What year's
    that?" and "That thing is *clean!*" and sometimes just "All right!"

and "Right there, right there!" and I think, Funny, nobody yells
        stuff like that when I'm in my 2006 Prius. What's the deal
with old cars? Or any car, really. Dorsey Dixon wrote
    "Wreck on the Highway" in 1936, the year when Ford came

came out with a V-8 engine and more people began to die
        all over the nation. More power, more uncertainty;
more uncertainty, more art. You can cheat somebody
    with a car: Sam Phillips promised a brand-new Cadillac

to the first Sun Records artist to write a hit song, which
        Carl Perkins did with "Blue Suede Shoes," though
the car was bought out of Carl's royalties. Before Zelda
    Fitzgerald married, she rode around in the back seats

of convertibles, and when she passed a group of boys, known
        as "jelly beans," she'd laugh, stretch her arms wide,
and cry, "All my jellies!" She made a king of Scott,
    at least for a while: together they put flesh on the spirit

of the era he would call the Jazz Age. And then it all
        went wrong. What happened? All we know is that Scott
wrote in a notebook, "I knew something had happened
    that could never be repaired." It was as though, having

eaten from every tree in the garden, they turned to the one
                that was forbidden to them, and when they ate of it,
they heard the voice of the Lord God walking in the garden
                in the cool of the day, and they hid themselves from

the presence of the Lord God among the trees of the garden,
                and the Lord God called to the man and said to him,
Where are you? and the man said, *I heard your voice*
                in the garden, and I was afraid, because I was naked,

so I hid myself, and the Lord God said, *Who told you*
                you were naked? In Paris, the Fitzgeralds meet Picasso,
Cole Porter, Fernand Léger, John Dos Passos, Hemingway,
                though when Scott kneels at Isadora Duncan's feet in

a restaurant near St. Paul de Vence and she runs her fingers
                through his hair, Zelda throws herself down a stairwell;
later, she collects jewelry from guests at a party and throws
                it into a pot of boiling water "to make soup," tosses her

clothes into a bathtub and sets fire to them, buys a gigantic
                gilt mirror, has a barre installed in front of it, and practices
ten hours a day, seven days a week, to "The Parade
                of the Wooden Soldiers," which Scott says later is engraved

on every organ of his body. It was as though the Lord God
                said to him, *I will put enmity between you and the woman,*
and to her, *I will multiply your sorrow,* and to them both,
                Cursed is the ground, thorns also and thistles shall it bring

forth, and in the sweat of your face shall you eat bread
                          until you return to the ground, for out of it you were taken,
for you are dust, and to dust shall you return. Where did
          Adam and Eve go when God drove them out of the garden?

Genesis tells us only that they were farmers, so you have
                          to imagine a little town with one stoplight, a store or two,
and what else: Camels? Arabs? Were there even Arabs
          then? Maybe a policeman in a cart pulled by a mule;

he'd go from hut to hut to make sure everybody was okay,
                          pull somebody in if they coveted somebody else's wife
or livestock or simply drank too much wine or beer,
          since hard liquor wouldn't come along for centuries.

Scott Fitzgerald dies at forty-four; he'd given up drinking
                          a year earlier but collapses while eating a Hershey bar.
Zelda outlives him by eight years but burns to death
          in an asylum fire while awaiting electroshock treatment,

as much in love with Scott as ever. Years earlier, they'd
                          rented an estate with enormous rooms on the Delaware
River, and Zelda ordered custom-made, oversized chairs
          and couches that made the people sitting in them look like

children—one day you're riding around in a convertible
                          shouting "All my jellies!" and then, like that, you're
wearing a dress that hasn't fit you in twenty years,
          and your face looks as though it's carved out of wood,

and you look like a doll someone propped up with
               a couple of cushions, and your feet don't even touch
the floor. Tooling around Memphis in Tad Pierson's
        '55 Cadillac and looking for the house where young

Isaac Hayes learned to play his grandmother's piano,
             it's hard not to think of all the wrong turns you've made
and the ones you have to make still. On the drive up
       from Montgomery, there are billboards saying God Has a Plan

For You, My Way or The Highway, Do You Know Where You're
            Going, Let's Meet at My House. And there you are in your
goddamn big car, as Robert Creeley says in his poem "I Know
      a Man," the one Robert Hass would call *the* poem of the fifties,

and you're in a rush, all you want to do is get safely down
            the road, yet there's darkness all around you, so you say to
your friend, *What can we do?* and he says to you, *Drive,*
      he says, and then *for Christ's sake watch where you're going.*

ODE TO DISAPPOINTMENT

Our guide Leyla says "don't be disappointed" before we go
to Troy, and when I say I understand there's not much there,
        she says, "Thank God for this one, Mr. David—I believe
    some of your fellow countrymen are expecting to see Brad Pitt,

        not to mention Orlando Bloom, Eric Bana, and other stars
of the celebrated if not very excellent 2004 Hollywood movie!"
        But that's America for you: travelers to Paris never
    never believe me when I tell them the Bastille was torn down,

        or if they do, they assume it's for the same reason we tear
things down here at home, that is, to put a McFriendly's in its place.
        There's no reason to get all worked up over it, though:
    "Should I kill myself or have a cup of coffee?" asks novelist Albert

        Camus. Have a cup of coffee, Albert! You can always kill
yourself later. You can always read philosopher Gaston Bachelard,
        who says the truest thing: Bachelard says
    we always begin in joy and end by organizing our disappointment,

        that whereas the moment of discovery is always fresh
and unfiltered, the moment of organization is when we
        exchange the pleasure we get from experiencing
    something for the pleasure we get from thinking about it. Boy,

        does that ever sound French! It also sounds very much like
what I do when I write a poem, but it sounds as well like my thoughts
        on the last overpriced restaurant meal I ate,
    not to mention the American political system, which is the point:

we take off from one place, then we're all over the map,
and now, because we're earnest and fundamentally decent
and have been up a time or two before,
we're bringing that thought in for a nice soft landing. Troy really

is pretty awful: it's like your backyard, assuming your
backyard is full of rocks and gulleys and the odd historical plaque
here and there. Who cares? Here is where
the Greeks clash with the Trojans, I say as I pound my chest, here

where Patroclus falls, then Hector, where the arrows
of Hercules rain down and the hammer of Ajax drives men into the ground
like tent pegs! After we walk all over the ruins
of the ancient city—which is raggedy, yes, but nobody ever said it was

small—we repair with Leyla to the restaurant just outside,
and as we attack our excellent Turkish lunches, suddenly
Leyla looks up and says, "Ha, ha—look,
there's Helen!" and sure enough, a blonde maiden is walking through

the parking lot, someone from Latvia, I'm guessing,
or the Czech Republic, and she looks a little sad,
and when she enters the restaurant
and sits, it is at the table of a man close to twice her age, her father,

perhaps, though I'm thinking that, if she is Helen,
the older man might be her Menelaus, which explains why
she is out of countenance, and as we tuck
into our lamb and pilaf and peppers and eggplant, I wonder

if somewhere a Paris is waiting, not in the city
of the same name but in Riga or Prague, and he's at a sidewalk café,
eating a pierogi or whatever they eat there, though
actually he's not eating at all, he's so lovesick, but is drinking

instead cup after cup of black coffee, and he's thinking
of how he kissed her that one time before she left for Troy,
how he put his hands on her hips and she hers
on his shoulder and he gave her a sort of tentative, is-this-okay kiss,

and she reacted, like, yeah, it's more than okay, and then,
poof, she's gone, as in out of his life forever if he doesn't
do something, only here he is in Prague
or Riga, and the waiter comes by and says Something wrong

with the pierogis, and he says No, I'm just not hungry
and throws down a handful of coins and hails a taxi, and the cabbie
says Where to, buddy? and he says,
The train station and then No, the airport, and make it fast.

YOU'VE BUILT YOUR OWN MOSQUE

When I read that architect Sinan had left a message
in a bottle telling restorers how to build again the arches
              of the mosque that he knew would
fall into decay, I thought, maybe I should do that for my poems—

       not because poets 400 years from now will want to write
poems like mine the way architects 400 years from then
              would want to build mosques like
Sinan's, but so I can know how to write those poems myself, starting,

       say, tomorrow morning, since most days I feel as though
poem writing is something I've never actually done
              before and certainly don't know
how to begin doing today, that is, tomorrow morning. Here's the story:

       in the early nineties, an engineer in Istanbul was trying
to figure out how to fix the crumbling doorway
              to Sinan's mosque but couldn't because
it had been built with sixteenth-century stone masonry techniques

       that no one understood, and finally he decided
to just take out the keystone and start there, but when
              the keystone came out, so did
a glass bottle containing a note from Sinan saying, "The lifetime

       of these stones that make this arch is 400 years. After
this period, they will be decayed and you will try
              to replace them. Probably architectural
techniques will also change and you won't be aware of our style.

That's why I wrote this letter to you," and then Sinan
talks about the stones in detail and tells where to find
                them in Anatolia and how to build
the arch again. Now there's foresight for you, not to mention

        public spiritedness, amity, comity, cordiality, and
friendship toward a bunch of people you haven't
                even met yet. There's an artist
who is doing what artists should, that is, putting other people first

        rather than obsessing over his desire to say what's
on his mind, whatever that is. I'd like to be able
                to write poems that way,
for you should be able to walk into a poem the way you walk into

        the garden of a mosque and smell the flowers, listen
to birdsong and the beautiful gurgling of the fountain,
                nod to others and receive their
smiles and nods in return. The sculptor Claes Oldenburg wrote,

        "I am for the art that a kid licks after peeling away
the wrapper. . . . I am for an art that is put on and
                taken off, like pants, which
develops holes, like socks, which is eaten, like a piece of pie."

        Me, too, Claes Oldenburg! If someone from the future
were to ask me how to write a poem, I'd advise
                that person to buy an ice
cream cone and enjoy it, and if he or she drops it on the sidewalk,

why, so much the better. I'd suggest you shop for new
underwear and take a taxi, or if you've taken a lot
              of taxis lately, walk to your
destination instead. If you take your pants off and put them on again

          and really pay attention, I'd say you could learn as much
about writing poetry as you could from reading a lot
              of poems, especially bad ones.
Why not help a kid blow her nose? Why not eat a hamburger sandwich

          or a slice of cake or both? Why not teach yourself how to
flap like a flag or grow holes the way socks do? I'd like
              a baked potato, please, with a pat
of melting butter on it, though given the choice, I wouldn't know which

          it would be better to be, the potato or the butter, and the same
goes for any poem that I wrote on that topic, that it
              be more like one or the other,
as each is necessary. I wouldn't want to begin smoking cigarettes

          or for you to, either, presuming you don't do so already,
which, if you do, you should stop doing, because
              it isn't good for you and will
make the people who love you unhappy. But you could write a poem

          that might be smoked like a cigarette or even one that
smells the way old shoes do, because smoke and foul
              odors are as much a part
of life as clear skies and the perfume of the tea olive, and by now surely

you can say, as Claes Oldenburg does, "I am for an art that
takes its form from the lines of life, that twists and extends
impossibly and accumulates
and spits and drips and is sweet and stupid as life itself."

There you are—you've edged the sidewalk and put
your tools away and made a pot of gumbo
and showed a kid how
to tie a Windsor knot in a necktie. You've built your own mosque,

and now you're inviting everyone in to see
how beautiful it is; even better, you've left
a message for people
who won't be born for 400 years. Make jam from the figs

on the tree in your own yard, bathe the dog and the cat, too,
if you can. Look what you've done. Isn't it magnificent?
You've already written
the poem—all you have to do now is get it down on paper.

GET UP, PLEASE

The two musicians pour forth their souls abroad
            in such an ecstasy as to charm the audience
       like none I've ever seen before, and when
they finish, they rise and hug each other,
           and then the tabla player bends down
and touches the feet of the santoor player in an obvious gesture

of respect, but what does it mean? I don't find out
            until the next day at the Econolodge in Tifton, GA,
       where I stop on my way home after the concert
and ask Mrs. Patel, the owner, if she has ever heard
           of these two musicians or knows
anything about the tabla and the santoor and especially the latter,

which looks like the love child of a typewriter
            and a hammered dulcimer only with a lot of extra wires
       and tuning posts, and she doesn't seem to understand
my questions, though when I ask her about one person touching
           the other's feet and then bend down
to show her, she lights up and says, "It means he thinks the other

is a god. My children do this before they go off
            to school in the morning, as though to say, 'Mummy,
       you are a god to us,'" and I look at her
for a second and then surprise us both when I say, "Oh, Mrs. Patel!"
           and burst into tears, because I think,
first, of my own dead parents and then of little Lakshmi and Padma

Patel going off to their classes in Tift County schools,
            the one a second-grader who is studying homophones
       ("I see the sea") and the other of whom is in the fourth

grade, where she must master long division with
                   its cruel insistence on numbers lined
up under one another with exacting precision and then crawling

toward the page's bottom as you, the divider, subtract
                   and divide again and again, all the while recording
           on the top line an answer that grows increasingly
lengthy as you fret and chew the tip of your pencil
                   and persevere, though before they grab
their books and lunch boxes and pile onto the bus, they take time

to touch Mrs. Patel's feet and Mr. Patel's as well,
                   assuming there is such a person. Later my friend
           Avni tells me you touch the feet of your elders
to respect the distance they have traveled
                   and the earth they have touched, and you
say "namaste" not because you take yoga at that little place

on the truck route between the t-shirt store
                   and the strip club but because it means "I bow
           to the light within you," and often the people being
bowed to will stoop down and collect you as if to say
                   "You too are made of the same light!"
Reader, if your parents are alive, think of them now, of all the gods

whose feet you never touched or touched enough.
                   And if not your parents, then someone else.
           You know someone like this, right? Someone who belongs
to the "mighty dead," as Keats called them.
                   Don't you wish that person were here now
so you could touch their feet and whisper, "You are my god"?

I can't imagine Keats saying, "You too are made
                of the same light," though I can see him saying,
        as he did to Fanny Brawne, "I have been astonished
that Men could die Martyrs for religion—I have
                shudder'd at it—I shudder no more—I could
be martyr'd for my Religion—Love is my religion—I could die for that—

I could die for you." My own feet have touched
                the earth nearly three times as long as Keats's did,
        and I'm hardly the oldest person
I know. So let this poem brush across the feet of anyone
                who reads it. Poetry is
my religion—well, I wouldn't die for it. I'd live for it, though.

JOHN THE CONQUEROR

In the kitchen, the women are saying things I don't
          understand: *He was as mad as a mule chewing bumblebees,*
    she's as happy as a dead pig in the sunshine, you're so
stuck up you'd drown in a rainstorm. And they'd talk
          about other women, like my mother's Aunt Julia,
    who wasn't her real aunt but who worked in my grandfather's

house for years, ministering to the farm animals
          and the humans, too, when they had a touch
    of the dropsy or just weren't feeling well. And once
the women were talking about another woman, one
          they knew, or it might have been a woman in a song,
    and she was a big woman, and she'd done something

only big women do or maybe something that all women
          do, though she'd done it in such a big way that she'd
    been arrested, but when her case came up, she *shook it*
so fine for the judge that he let her go and sent the cops
          to jail, and while I didn't know what *shook it* meant
    or even what *it* was, I knew the women in the kitchen

were talking about something more powerful
          than anything I'd come across yet in my short life,
    something I'd find out about later, when I was a man,
if then. Aunt Julia wore two corsets, the one to do
          what any corset does and the other to hold all the plants
    and shoots in her backwoods pharmacy, from the alfalfa

leaf that prevents poverty to the tonka beans that stop
          your enemy's heart and the white sage that keeps your
    enemy from stopping yours, and of these, there was none

more powerful than the herb the women called John
　　　　　the Conqueror that would make the one you love
　　　love you and that took its name from an African prince

　　　who was sold as a slave, though his spirit was never
　　　　　broken, and who survives in folklore as a trickster
　　　of the type who appears in the works of the Zora Neale
Hurston who said he is like King Arthur of England,
　　　　　that is, not dead at all but waiting to return when
　　　his people call him. Late in life, the Freud who called himself

　　　a godless Jew embraced monotheism because belief
　　　　　in many gods meant you had to invoke a hundred of them
　　　every day to banish spells, open locked boxes, get a man's
attention, win at cards. No, no, better to believe in a single
　　　　　deity, as the Jews do; this allowed them to see
　　　the Big Picture, Freud said, and make advances in difficult fields

　　　like law and medicine. John the Conqueror, if I had to pick
　　　　　one god, it'd be you. Not only would you lead me to love
　　　but you'd also help me avoid the bad love that can look
like good love until it's too late. And you'd help me love
　　　　　myself as much as did the mother of, yes, the Sigmund
　　　Freud who said there was no advantage in life greater

　　　than being the first-born male child of a Jewish mother, who,
　　　　　in his case, dandled him on her knee and called him *mein
　　　goldener Sigi.* My golden Siggy: what words could be
sweeter on a child's ear? In the kitchen, the women laugh
　　　　　about their own mothers and how old-fashioned
　　　they were and how they'd complain about the women's friends,

30

whom they considered "fast," and say things like
        Look at her, she's putting on that beauty makeup
   and *She's just wearing that brassiere so her bosoms*
will stick out and men will look at her
        and *You bait a trap with meat,*
    honey, and you ain't gonna catch nothing but a dog.

John the Conqueror, you're my Jewish mother.
        You're my Aunt Julia. You're my big woman,
   even though you're a man. In the kitchen,
the women say *You can put a cat in an oven,*
        but it won't lay biscuits. They say
    Why are you smiling like a goat in a briar patch,

    he's as useful as a screen door on a submarine,
        her pants were so tight I could see her religion.
   John, there have been times in my life when
I might have called you out of the swamp,
        watched you step past
    the sleeping birds until you reached me and took my hand.

Where are we going? You don't even know what I want.
        Out on the lake, we hear the loon's cry, long
   and mournful; it says, *I'm here—where are you?* You start
to speak, and I don't know what you're saying, but I think
        you mean *wait, wait, listen,* and then,
    sure enough, from the other shore, there's an answer.

ODE TO LISTS

"Lyndon," writes presidential secretary Evelyn Lincoln just
        hours after her boss has been shot in Dallas, and this on
the plane that carries not only Jack Kennedy's remains but
      also Lyndon Johnson himself, seated just a few rows away
        and unaware that he is the first in a list of figures she thinks
responsible for the assassination. Surely she covered her

notebook with an in-flight magazine or said, "Oh, nothing"
        when the now-president asked her what she was doing as
he passed her on his way to comfort Mrs. Kennedy or just go
      to the bathroom, but it wouldn't have made much difference
        if he had seen it—granted, to be named as the number one
suspect in a presidential assassination is probably not

something he dreamed about in high school, but since the list
        ends with "Dictators" and "Communists," it seems more
a hysterical outpouring of grief on Evelyn Lincoln's part
      than anything to worry about; his plate's full already with
        everything on *his* list, all the good stuff (the Great Society
programs) as well as the bad (Vietnam). Every list is a poem,

which doesn't mean it's a good poem, although many are, like
        Nabokov's names for Lolita's classmates, which includes
saintly names like Grace Angel and sinister ones like
      Aubrey McFate. Then there are all the synonyms for
        "drunk" compiled by H. L. Mencken, among them
snooted, stewed, jugged, jagged, and pifflicated. When

he listed the four most overrated things in life, Christopher
        Hitchens said champagne, lobster, anal sex, and picnics,
though when this was repeated at his memorial service,

Stephen Fry said, "Well, three out of four isn't bad."
            Who knew that Stephen Fry doesn't like champagne?
You'd think all English people like champagne;

they certainly drink enough of it in the movies. I'm sure
            they like lists as much as the rest of us, though,
and see their utility: when the test pilot was flying a jet
            alone at 30,000 feet and there was a leak in his oxygen
                mask, he passed out and came to at 15,000 feet, and even
though he was groggy, he still told himself, *Cut the throttle*

and punch the dive brakes, cut the throttle and punch
                the dive brakes, which he did until the plane leveled out
at 5,000 feet instead of auguring into a schoolhouse
            or old folks' home. Two items is awfully short for a list,
                but my wife says there are only two things she doesn't
understand, dodgeball and limoncello, which I kind of

like, and not only because she's my wife: dodgeball leads
                people who you thought were friends to pretend to hate
you, which can lead to real hate, and limoncello has
            an alcohol content high enough to make its imbibers merry
                yet is sickly sweet, and since alcohol's main effect is
to make you drink more alcohol, more limoncello leads to

a heart high-sorrowful and cloy'd, a burning forehead,
            and a parching tongue, effects produced also though
in less intensity and duration by craft beer, vodka,
            and chardonnay. Long lists are silly, like those "37 Ways to
                Drive Your Man Wild in Bed" ones—what right-minded
fellow wants to lie there, dreaming of the pleasures to come,

only to have some naked tart straddle him with a clipboard
                in one hand and a Pilot G-2 Fine Point pen in the other!
No, no, keep your lists short, especially ones pertaining
        to human relations, for that way you will stand a better
                chance of remembering them. Parents of small children,
tell them they can't say "Yuck!" in response to anything

on their plate, and they must take at least one bite
                of everything. Parents of older children, say you
have to make the best grades you're capable of and
        be mannerly, in school and out. What is not a list?
                "I love you" is two pronouns and a verb, yet it has brought
more pleasure than any longer list, also more trouble.

OH, WELL

It's delicious, your cheese sandwich, just wonderful,
even though there's something a little unusual about the cheese,
     a little off, and that's when you realize you didn't take
out the sheet of paper that separates one slice from another, and now
     the only thing to do is take your whole sandwich apart,

     putting the tomato slices, the arugula, the avocado to one side
and separating the cheese and discarding that portion of the paper
     you haven't already chewed and swallowed, and then
you'll have to put the whole thing together again and go into the kitchen
     and wash and dry your hands, and during that time, the wide

     receiver will have caught the pass in the end zone, the power
forward will have leapt into the air and drilled the ball through
     the hoop, the chukka will have ended, and now the players
are cantering about laughing, their mallets slung casually
     over their shoulders, and you will have no idea what has happened,

     whether the ball has been driven fairly through your or the other
team's goal or blocked by a hook, a bump, a ride-off. Or
     you press down on your stapler only to discover that it's empty,
and it's been so long since you've had to refill it that you can't
     remember where the staples are, and then you do! There's a box

     of a thousand in the drawer on the left, but when you open it,
you remember that was in another desk in the house you used
     to live in, and that was years ago. You put on your pants
and realize the button is missing, and these are the only pants
     that go with the shirt you're already wearing, and while it's easy

to sew a new button on, you don't have one, and there are none
in the little sewing kit you got the last time you stayed at a hotel,
        which is not so bad, really, because someone has used the black
and brown thread, and all that's left is the red and the green,
        but your pants are too new to throw away, so you fold them

        and put them away, even though you know you'll forget
and take them out three more times and say, "Huh, no button"
        before giving them to Goodwill, St. Vincent de Paul,
the Salvation Army. Now you pick up that perfect apple,
        the one that's rock-hard, its shiny red shot through with

        yellow and green, like every other great apple you've
ever eaten, and you bite down, and rather than a crisp,
        exhilarating tartness, you end up with a mouthful of mealy crap,
and you think, if I put that much hope in an apple—an apple!—
        then imagine the real letdowns that await you, that open

        the door to an empty universe, one filled, so to speak,
with utter despair and nihilism, that destroy your happiness,
        convince you that life is a sham, a fraud, a hoax. At work,
you hate yourself for wanting a snack from the vending
        machine, but you put your money in anyway and make

        your choice, and the spiral turns, and your snack comes
halfway out of its dock and sticks there, and for a moment
        you want to smash your head through the glass and bleed
to death on the cashews, the pretzels, all the candy you never
        see sold in stores because only a starving person in a workplace

would buy it, and then you think how stupid you'd look,
how everyone who saw you before the ambulance came
would take a cellphone photo that would make its way
onto the social media and stay there for years, so you dig
into your pocket for more change because now you're going

to pay twice for your fruit pie, cheese crackers, granola bar,
and your hand goes down past your keys, past your pocket calculator,
all the way to the hole in the bottom, and that's when you
remember, yes, my bus fare fell through that hole this morning, which is
why I had to walk to work, just as I'll walk home, footsore

and hungry. Or you have a car, after all, but it's raining,
and your umbrella is in the back seat, and you can see your car
from your office, and the windows are open. On the way home,
you shift from side to side on the seat like a kid ashamed
of her cold wet diaper, and you stop at the store, and finally

you get to the front of the line, and all your stuff's on the counter,
and you reach for your buy-one-get-two-free coupon, but you
can't find it, and that means either you'll pay for all three
or have to tell the cashier that actually you never wanted even
one of the damned things, much less three of them. You tilt

your glass of wine to your lips while checking your Facebook
messages, and it's empty. An hour into your movie, your DVD
freezes, and you take the disc out and blow on it. Did you really
think you could fix it by blowing on it? On the other hand,
your car did start this afternoon; it got you home, so it works,

and your phone, and there's always basic cable. Animals
like you—well, animals like everybody, but at least they don't
        make an exception in your case. And you'll find someone
some day. People are always hooking up with people they
        knew in high school; why not you? There's always takeout.

THE JUGGLER OF NOTRE-DAME

"Very few men know how to take a walk," says Dr. Johnson.
    Well, I'm not one of them, your honor! Though it is hardly
  I who is responsible for the excellence of my perambulations

and more likely the neighborhood itself in which said
    perambulations are taken, where one meets, for example,
  Fritz the schnauzer, the same Fritz who rushes at me every

time as though to rip my throat out, and then he pauses,
    lowers his jaw, stares at me in amazement, and then leaps
  into my arms and licks my face as though to say, "It's him!

It's him!" Or Stanley, the orange tabby who spends his days
    napping in the middle of the street yet never gets run over,
  or Oliver and Archibald, two cats who are indistinguishable

until Archibald climbs you as though you were a tree
    and drapes himself around your neck like a fur stole
  while Oliver sniffs and licks himself and looks off into

the distance as though to say, "Brother? What brother?
    I don't have any brother." How like these animals are
  to the juggler of legend, the itinerant artist named Jean

who can't make a living by practicing his art, so he
    becomes a monk and enters a monastery where the other
  monks include a clarinettist, percussionist, and flautist,

each of whom has composed an elaborate instrumental to play
    before a statue of the Virgin, though when it is Jean's turn
  to perform, he has only his juggling to offer. *Sacrilege!*

cry the other monks. *Sacrilege!* But suddenly the Virgin
        comes to life and extends her arms toward Jean, now deep
    in prayer. *A miracle!* cry the others. A miracle! And that

is my cry as well when I am greeted on my walk by
        one or more of my four-legged friends, each of whom
    has nothing to offer me except his silliness, a gift

so Lilliputian as to be unworthy of the name "gift"
        and therefore unlikely ever to be stocked at the finer
    jewelry stores on the Place Vendôme of Paris

or New York's Fifth Avenue, places largely patronized,
        as far as I can tell, almost entirely by wealthy men buying
    diamond clips, lockets, amulets, thumb rings, fascinators,

and breastplates to distract either wives who've just
        learned of the existence of their mistresses or mistresses
    who've just learned that the men really have no intention

of leaving their wives, although the face licks of these
        animals, their very waddles and rump-shakings and even
    the scratches they bestow on me as they express their love

are more to me than any gold bracelet, sapphire pendant,
        ruby brooch. From here it's on past the Indian restaurant
    where I went one night with three friends to celebrate

the book one of them had just published and where we were
        treated to drinks by the owner, whose name was Bupendra
    but who was quite drunk and said we could call him Bob.

Next is the barber shop where all the barbers are either
  ex-military or ex-law enforcement or both and which
  is therefore patronized by every uniform in town and fully

half of the plainclothesmen, including the governor's
  security detail as well as the police who patrol every ball
  game, supermarket opening, cotillion, christening,

cremation, bar mitzvah, and boat launch in the area
  and who therefore know everything that is going to happen
  before anyone else does, including but not limited to deaths,

divorces, bankruptcies, indictments, sex changes, and ménage
  à trois. Whew! What a long walk this is becoming.
  Dr. Johnson never warned us—maybe this is why

so few people start. It's enough to make a walker feel a little
  peckish, so it's just as well that the fried chicken shack
  is where it has been for the last thirty-five years, making

it possible for one to get their signature sandwich, that is,
  a chicken breast on a bun with mayonnaise, mustard,
  and pickle from, not Gladys and Darlene, the two old

darlings who worked there for most of those thirty-five years
  and have been replaced by two younger women (actually,
  any woman would be younger than either Gladys or Darlene)

whose names one has not learned yet. Now to wash that down
  with something from the coffee shop whose owner always
  seems to be on the verge of committing homicide or suicide

or both, perhaps because he has sampled too many iterations
            of *his* signature offering, a hot chocolate with four shots
      of espresso in it, which calming beverage is named for

singer/songwriter Keith Richards of the Rolling Stones.
            But the sun is everywhere today, and not the harsh sun
      that pounds the earth like a hammer but a sun that is more

like a laughing boy or young suitor, his boater flying off
            his head as he chases the girls to kiss them—who needs
      caffeine? "The gloom of the world is but a shadow,"

said Fra Giovanni Giocondo in 1513. "Behind it, yet within
            our reach, is joy. Take joy." I will, you good Italian holy man!
      For you tell us that life gives freely, but we, judging its gifts

by their appearance, often cast them away as ugly or heavy
            or hard. "Remove the covering, and you will find beneath it
      a living splendor. . . . Welcome it, grasp it, and you touch

the angel's hand that brings it to you." There are gifts everywhere:
            why, even the coffee shop owner's anger is a gift, for surely
      his coffee would not be so excellent if he were a smiling idiot

who loves himself so much that he serves substandard fare
            to us, his customers, assuming that it is enough for us merely
      to be in the presence of his totally baseless self-approval.

Accounts by some of the thousands of Christian warriors
            who looked out on the Muslim fleet at the Battle of Lepanto
      reflect the writers' certain knowledge that many of them

will die that day, though at that moment, they all marvel
            at the beauty of the enemy's ships, their sails of red
        and orange and silver spread from one end of the horizon

to the other. In the Cathedral of Notre-Dame, a light
            envelops the Virgin, angels surround her, celestial voices
        are heard, and the juggler dies. Why not, though? "The whole gift

of the day" is passed from bird to bird, writes Pablo Neruda.
            Okay, but it's cat to cat in my neighborhood, Pablo!
        Though the birds are doing their part, mainly by staying

out of the cats' way. Stanley, Oliver, Archibald, Gladys,
            Darlene, even the angry coffee shop guy whose name
        I won't mention because he might see this poem

and refuse to let me drink his excellent coffee:
            every day they pull aside the thick curtain of this world
        and look, there's the night, beautiful and the bluest blue.

THE MINOTAUR

How ugly is the Minotaur, with the head and tail of a bull
and the body of a man between! And how angry he is,
   if for good reason: like all of us, he never asked
to be born, especially as the love child of Pasiphae,
   King Minos's wife, who fell in love with a snow-white

bull sent to Minos by Poseidon for sacrifice, though when
the king coveted the bull for himself, the sea god took
   revenge by having Pasiphae not only fall in love with
the creature but commission a wooden cow from
   Daedalus so she could climb inside and then, well,

you know. Hardly bears thinking about, right, reader?
And just imagine the actual birth: think "bull," then think
   "horns." Ouch! Anyway, Minos takes one look
at the Minotaur and calls Daedalus back and says,
   "Daedalus, build me a labyrinth and put the Minotaur

inside so he can't menace anyone except for the seven
youths and maidens we'll let him devour every nine
   years, and while you're at it, lock yourself up in a tower
so you can't give away the secret of the labyrinth."
   You know what happens next: Daedalus makes

wings for himself and his son Icarus, and off they go—
well, off goes Daedalus, since Icarus soars too high
   and melts the wax that holds his wings together
and plunges into the sea, leaving the Minotaur to beat
   his horns against the walls of his prison as he waits

for the youths and maidens to appear so he can devour
them and go back to starving for another nine years.
        But anger issues aside, wouldn't you want to be
the Minotaur, as wise as a man yet possessed of
        the strength of a bellowing, butting, snorting, kicking

        bull? A web site I just consulted said a bull's "threat
display" consists of an arched back followed by
        a lowered head, protrusion of the eyeballs, and erection
of the hair along the back. How about trying that
        during a bar fight, say, or an English Department

        faculty meeting? And what about you ladies: don't
you ladies like it when we fellows are full of swagger
        and confidence, as long as we don't go overboard?
You certainly wouldn't want to be Daedalus,
        although Professor George Francis FitzGerald

        of Trinity College, Dublin, did: in 1895, FitzGerald tried
to replicate the great architect's feat, rising to a height
        of only six inches before crashing; authorities say thirteen-
year-old James Joyce may have witnessed the attempt,
        which surely got him to thinking about time, memory,

        the past, confinement and freedom, consciousness,
existence, and other top-shelf literary themes.
        So who tries to replicate the feats of the Minotaur?
I'll tell you who: every man who gazes upon the body
        of the woman he loves, that's who. And the women

like it as well, or at least they like it when the man
part and the bull part balance each other out,
            with the bull getting things started and the man
applying the finesse or, as Mr. Collins says in *Pride*
            and Prejudice in an entirely different context,

            offering "those little delicate compliments
which are always acceptable to ladies,"
            though it's the minotaur who takes over
for the grand finale with all of its whooping
            and yelling and throwing of bedclothes

            hither and thither and then the man again for
the dénouement with its cooing and caressing
            and reassurance that that was wonderful, you're
wonderful, of course I'll call you, of course, of course.
            A study by psychology professor Marta Meana

            says "women want a caveman and caring," in
the professor's words. "Women want to be thrown
            up against a wall but not truly endangered."
When I tell women in their twenties about this,
            they get angry, but when I mentioned it recently

            to a fifty-year-old, she said, Sounds good to me.
Okay, I've got it. What you want to be is the Minotaur
            but not say you are: you can't just sit down next to
somebody in a bar and say, "Hi, I'm the Minotaur"
            and expect her to say, "Hi, I'm Debbie,

your place or mine?" No, you say, "Hi, I'm Bob,"
and she says, "Pleased to meet you, Bob," and you buy
          her a drink and ask her what her work is, and soon
she's talking about herself, just jabbering away,
          and she doesn't even notice that you're leaning in

          a little, and your head's lower than it was, and your eyes
are sort of shiny, and when she says something about her job
          or her pets or her hobbies and you make
an "uh-huh" of assent, though it's starting to get breathier,
          more like an "ummh-hummh!" than an "uh-huh."

          And then she notices all this, and she likes it.
And the next thing you know, she's scratching
          your ears. Then she holds out her hand,
and there's a sugar cube, and you lick it
          off her palm, and yeah, she really likes that.

COME TO FIND OUT

That's what my mother and her sisters used to say
on the porch late at night when they thought I wasn't
listening: *He said he had to travel so much because*
        his job was in sales, but come to find out he had a wife
   and a whole other family in Breaux Bridge or *He said*
he was a captain and got wounded in the war; come to
        find out he never rose above private and damn sure

        never saw active service, excuse my French.
Come to Find Out meant that something was going
to be revealed and in that way was a cousin to All Is
        Not As It Seems and One Thing Led to Another,
   which suggests that the second thing reveals or
in some way at least echoes the first. And then there
        was What Was I Thinking, the answer to which

        was almost always You Weren't, though sometimes
   you were: *She's not very bright so I'll have my way*
with her or *He'll stay home and keep house and I'll pay*
        the bills or *Who needs health insurance.* What'd you
   think, those babies were going to feed
themselves and change their own diapers? Oh, if only
        life were like the opera, where you can say what

        you think about somebody while you're standing
   right next to them, yet they don't seem to hear you.
Actually, a better verb than "say" is "sing": apparently you can
        mouth the most wounding insults and get away without
   being slapped or stabbed as long as you dress them
in eighth-note triplets. Art says to us, What do you
        want to be true, and then it gives us all these choices:

you can do whatever you like or, if you prefer,
        nothing at all. No wonder some people hate it,
though I say, Thank you, art! Thank you, opera, plays,
                movies, things you hang on a wall or put on a pedestal!
        Thank you, poems of every length, from the *Inferno*
to a haiku, provided the haiku poet puts as much time
                into his or her poem as Dante put into his! Which seems

                unlikely, but we're trying to uphold standards here,
        right, reader? Thank you, symphony orchestras
and flash mobs—what could be better than going to
                your local Walmart to buy a sack of onions, some puppy
        biscuits, and a carton of smokes only to be surprised
by a guy pulling a sax out of a box and being joined
                by a woman with a bassoon, three string players,

                and a twenty-person chorus who launch into "Ode to Joy,"
        a 1785 Friedrich Schiller poem that becomes the final
movement of the Ninth Symphony by celebrated German
                composer/pianist Ludwig van Beethoven! It's 1796 now,
        and come to find out Beethoven's losing his hearing,
possibly from typhus, systemic lupus erythematosus,
                or even his habit of immersing his head in cold water

                to stay awake. He stops performing, though he continues
        to compose. He also avoids conversation. Talk is cheap!
He digs in, though, writes the Fifth Symphony that begins
                with the four most famous notes in musical history, notes
        that, as he himself said, sound like Fate knocking
at the door. Then another symphony and another
                and another still, till he writes the Ninth, the one whose

opening fanfare is said to have put a lump even
in Hitler's throat. Come to find out art works the same
way on everybody; you could be a pirate or a headsman
or the pope or the owner of a dry-cleaning establishment
and still laugh as Punch and Judy throw pots and pans
at each other, weep when the soprano sings
of the lover, the land, the mother she'll never see again.

Everybody's got a story, and half the time there's a story
behind the story, and in half of the cases that are like that,
we'll never know what it is. But you can go your whole
day without hearing any music at all, and then you can
talk to or buy a carton of tomatoes from or just pass by
somebody who has; one thing leads to another in this
world, and the next thing you know, you're happy.

LET'S TAKE OFF

You say to me, "Let's take off our clothes," and even though I say, "Let's!"
          I can't help thinking of how, in Rick Bragg's
      biography of Jerry Lee Lewis, the phrase
"take off" occurs again and again but in a different context, as in
          "Daddy pulled a knife on Chuck Berry, and Chuck took off"
      and "when I seen how big that fella was, I took
off," which in turn makes me think of the summer I worked on a road

crew in Houma and picked up everything from the guys I worked with
          that I wouldn't get from my professors at school.
      Most of it had to do with fighting: they'd say
"You done overshot your runway, son" or "If you ain't gonna
          be no bull, you shouldn't have bellowed" or "I'd rather
      sandpaper a bobcat's butt in a phone booth
than fight him." To get to and from work, we'd pack five or six fellows

into somebody's heap and listen to a country station on the way,
          where it was more of the same, or a soul
      station, where the DJs spun records for "all you flattop
cats and dungaree dolls," played Chuck Berry and Little Richard
          for "all the fingerpopping daddies and transistor sisters."
      If we're lucky and smart, we contain all of
the people we love; if we're dumb, it's the people we hate who shape us.

The good ones let us see ourselves not as we are but as we want to be.
          How did Shakespeare know so much when
      he was a kid from a town smaller than this one? Duke
Ellington said it was because he spent his days
          hanging around the pool hall, that the elements were
      so mixed in him that Nature might stand up and say to all
the world, as Antony does of Caesar, "This was a man." One night we were

on the edge of a bar fight that was getting out of hand, and one of the guys
         I worked with said, "Let's take off—
    I'd rather hear them say, 'Yonder he goes' than 'Don't he
look natural.'" Another time, the fellow who ran the crew
              said there were fourteen kids in his family and eleven
         of them had webs between their toes, and when
I asked him if that were true, he said, "I don't know" and then "Maybe."

Over time, things tend to take care of themselves. Yes, Jerry Lee's
              father caught up with Chuck Berry,
    but by then they were too tired to fight, so they talked it out,
and everyone saw them together in the hotel restaurant
              the next morning, having breakfast. We've got to get
         out of this place. I know, let's take off
our clothes, and after that, let's take off, if it's the last thing we ever do.

I HAD A GIRL

State Road 82, Port Arthur, Texas, 1961

Days after my friends and I found those dying boys
          on that Texas highway, I wondered if it had been like that
for Buddy Holly and Richie Valens when their plane went
          down outside of Clear Lake, Iowa
in 1959: the glass, the twisted metal, the boys like babies screaming

for their mothers, but no, they didn't die the way our boys
          did. Their plane hit the frozen ground so hard that they were
gone before they knew their lives were over. And then
          there was silence, a little wind,
a startled animal shivering in its lair until the sun came up hours

later and the search party arrived. Always the silence.
          Then a door slamming, a bell, footsteps: Buddy Holly
knocks Peggy Sue Gerron down as he rushes to an assembly
          where he's scheduled to play and doesn't
even stop to help her up, though he tells her over his shoulder that she has

beautiful lips, and it isn't until months later that Peggy Sue
          goes to a Buddy Holly concert and hears her name,
her song spooling out of the amplifiers as the band
          plays a tune first written
for Cindy Lou, Buddy's niece, but changed at the last minute so drummer

Jerry Allison, who was the boyfriend of Peggy Sue,
          from whom he'd parted recently, could get her back.
That same year, Donna Ludwig is dating Richie
          Valens, and he calls her one
night and sings the song he's written for her over the phone,

though she doesn't know it's a real song until she
              is riding around with her girlfriends one night,
and they turn on the car radio and hear, "I had a girl,
              Donna was her name. . . ."
"It was wonderful," says Donna thirty-five years later. She's a Sacramento

businesswoman now, and Peggy Sue is the co-owner of a plumbing
              company called Rapid Rooter in the same town, though
neither knows about the other. And one day Peggy Sue hears
              there's a real Donna behind the Richie
Valens song, so she calls her and says, "Is this Richie Valens' Donna?"

I was sixteen years old when my friends and I
              found those boys on that Texas highway.
The driver was dead already. Seats, windows,
              dashboard: everything
was painted with whiskey and blood. The other boys screamed

and wept. We couldn't touch them: their bones showed
              through their flesh. Their breath left them, and then
the silence again, and then a siren as an ambulance
              roars up and two medics
jump out, one turning aside in horror when he sees what we see.

Donna has gotten a lot of calls like this over the years,
              so she's a little wary. "Yes?" she says, and Peggy Sue
says, "Well, this is Buddy Holly's Peggy Sue."
              James Marsh's 1993
documentary on the two women ends with a TV commercial

for Rapid Rooter in which Donna says, "My drain was clogged,
        and by the time I got out of the shower
and blew my hair dry, there was a note on my door,
        thanking me for my business.
I'm recommending it to all my friends." And there's Peggy Sue, standing

next to a Rapid Rooter van. "When there's a plumbing problem,"
        she says, "we're here for you." Both women are in their
their fifties now. What have they learned? That you don't
        overdramatize. Everything can be
fixed. The important things are few. That silence is everywhere:

you come out of it, you go back in. And then you hear something,
        like an air brake on the highway or the wind that comes
down out of the mountain this time of year, though sharper,
        like a gasp. "What is that?" you say.
And then you know: it's the breath he took the first time he saw you.

A FEW OLD THINGS

Rilke said he wanted a room "with a few old things
            and a window opening onto great trees," which makes
me think of my favorite rooms and their furnishings,
        an obvious choice being this brightly lit bedroom,
            newspapers and coffee cups on the floor, bedclothes
scattered everywhere, perfumed with the smell
        of sex, maybe, or maybe not. And if not, okay;

    they've smelled of sex before and will again.
            Well, probably. As Fats Waller said, "One never
knows, do one?" Then there's the kitchen with
        a pizza in a blazing oven, perhaps, or a risotto
            bubbling while you chop salad and blast Big Jack
Johnson on a pair of tinny speakers. Then it's off
        to the dining room and Chopin while you eat

    your jambalaya or cassoulet or whatever it was
            you cooked, and now the living room, a fire
toppling as you sip eau de vie and toy with a cigar
        and listen to Penderecki's Symphony no. 3,
            the one he wrote for the war dead, the words sung
by soprano Dawn Upshaw, whose voice enters
        the music so gradually that you don't realize

    someone is singing until she all but cries out in joy
            or terror, you're not sure which. Now you're
in the space between image and idea where Keats
        spent his happiest hours, skating back and forth
            between some old book in your hand
and your memories of other books, of things you did
        when you were a kid or even last week and things

other people told you they did, of your mother
            and father, lovers you might have
treated better and ones who might have been nicer to you,
            friends you broke with even though
                you can't remember a single one,
historical figures—silly ones, like Thomas Taylor
            the Platonist, who invented a "perpetual lamp" fueled

    by oil, salt, and phosphorus that exploded during
            his demonstration of it at the Freemasons'
Tavern in 1785 which, he noted ruefully, raised
        a prejudice against the device "which could never
            afterwards be removed," and merry ones, like
Don Juan of Austria, who, just before the battle
            of Lepanto, was seized by "a fit of exuberance

    beyond rational thought" and danced a galliard
            on the gun-platform of the command vessel
to the music of fifes. And all the while you're thinking
        of tomorrow and of the things you have to do
            and the ones you want to do, and you wonder
if it'd be better to have a list to make sure you don't
            forget anything or if it'd be better just to get up

    and start working and in that way do the thing you
            weren't expecting to do, the one that doesn't
appear on any list or even in your mind as you
        were dozing, waking, dozing again, the idea
            that enters you like a cry in the night—one minute
you're at a table in a tavern with your friends, it seems,
            and the next, you're in the street, saying, Now what?

IS SPOT IN HEAVEN?

In St. Petersburg, Sasha points and says, "They're restorating
this zoo building because someone is giving the zoo an elephant
        and the building is not enough big, so they are restorating it,"

so I say, "Where's, um, the elephant?" and Sasha says,
"The elephant is waiting somewhere! How should I know!"
        When I was six, my dog was Spot, a brindled terrier with

with the heart of a lion, though mortal, in the end, like all
of us, and when he died, I said to Father Crifasi, "Is Spot
        in heaven?" and he laughed and asked me if I were really

that stupid, insinuating that he, a holy father of the church,
had the inside track on heavenly entry, knew where
        the back stairs were, had mastered the secret handshake.

Later we saw a guy with a bear, and I said, "Look, a bear!"
and Sasha said, "Ah, the poor bear! Yes, you can have your
        picture with this one, if you like," but by then I didn't want to.

Who is in heaven? God, of course, Jesus and his mother,
and the more popular saints: Peter, Michael, the various
        Johns, Josephs, and Catherines. But what about the others?

If Barsenuphius, Frideswide, and Jutta of Kulmsee,
why not Spot or the elephant or the bear when it dies?
        Even a pig or a mouse has a sense of itself, said Leonard

Wolff, who applied this idea to politics, saying no single
creature is important on a global scale, though a politics
        that recognizes individual selves is the only one that offers

a hope for the future. Pets are silly, but the only world
worth living in is one that doesn't think so. As to the world
            beyond this one, as Sam Cooke says, I'm tired of living

            but afraid to die because I don't know what's coming next.
I do know that Spot was always glad to see me, turning
            himself inside out with joy when I came home from school,

            whereas Father Crifasi took no delight at the sight of me
or anyone, the little pleasure that sometimes hovered
            about his lips falling out of his face like a spark from

            a cigarette when the door to the classroom opened
and we boys filed in as slowly as we could. Those
            years are covered as by a mist now, the heads of my parents

            and friends breaking through like statues in a square
in a foreign city as the sun comes over my shoulder
            and the night creeps down cobblestoned streets toward

            a future I can't see, though across the river, it's still dark,
but already you can hear the animals stirring:
            the first birds, then an elephant, a bear, a little dog.

MRS. JONES

In high school, I'd wander down to the Home Ec room
after class because there were always girls there
    and something to eat. And Mrs. Jones, who always said
the same thing every time she saw me: "You're going
    to be a handsome man when you grow up, David Kirby!"

How would she know? She was thirty-five, maybe.
I was sixteen. Whatever became of Home Ec? It's now
    called Family Science, as if that were even possible.
Also Human Ecology, which makes more sense,
    since "ecology" just means the give and take of life:

I make the pie, you eat a slice, you thank me.
Somebody should write an opera about high school.
    How many musicals have been set there? I see myself
walking down to the Home Ec room. The door opens,
    and someone comes out. It's my young self, I think,

but he's going the other way, so I can't see, and I want
to ask if Mrs. Jones still teaches here, but he can't hear me,
    either. There's the sign, though: "Mrs. Mary Jones."
And there you are, Mrs. Jones, putting away the Mixmaster
    and hanging your apron on the back of the door.

I clear my throat so as not to startle you, but you jump
anyway, then say, *David Kirby! Is that you?* God,
    you're beautiful. How could I have thought you old?
The girls made a pound cake, you say. *Would you*
    like a piece? It's fall, and there's a whistle on

the football field. No, I don't want a piece of cake.
I just want to look at you, Mrs. Jones. You say,
    Call me Mary, silly! But I can't—you're a teacher.
You told me everything I needed to know about women,
    though it took me years to learn. I want to take you

    to dinner. I want to make love to you, but I'm twice
your age now, and besides, there's a Mr. Jones.
    I'd like to break his neck. I don't mean that. You deserve
to grow old with someone like yourself. I hope
    he's sweet to you. I bet he is. The light is creeping out

    of the sky the way it does this time of year, and it'll be
dark before we know it. The athletes laugh and shove
    each other as they make their way to the parking lot.
Soon there's just one car left. It's Coach Wilson's.
    We're playing Destrehan this weekend. They'll kill us.

    Still, Coach watches game film, draws his Xs and Os.
Maybe we'll win—maybe we'll get lucky this time.
    Another car pulls in, and a man gets out. You look
over my shoulder, Mrs. Jones, and your face lights up
    like the bonfire at the pep rally tomorrow before our boys

    take the field and lose again. *I better be going,* you say.
And look, I'm sixteen. I can do this, I think. The door
    opens, and a man walks in. *Are you David?* he says,
and when I tell him I am, he says, *A girl's waiting.*
    She asked me if I'd seen you. She wants a ride home.

GIRL GROUPS

The Crystals, the Ronettes, the Dixie Cups: who does not adore them?
    Who doesn't hear in those voices a love so warm,
so welcoming that you can rest your soul there?
    Often accused of being mere froth, girl-group songs
are anything but: it's 1964, and producer Jeff Barry
    is coaching Mary Weiss of the Shangri-Las through the end

of "The Leader of the Pack," and she's not quite getting it, so he says,
    "Look what happens to this guy. Here he is, he loves
this girl. And just think about her: she stands there and sees him pull away
    on his motorcycle for the last time," and by now,
Mary Weiss is sobbing, and when she screams,
    "Look out! Look out! Look out!" you hear the terror in her voice,

and you cry, too. "Everyone is going to hurt you," says Bob Marley,
    "you just got to find the ones worth
suffering for." Thing is, you don't know who you're going
    to fall in love with or where or when:
Dante tells us that Francesca da Rimini was
    married to Giovanni Malatesta, but he was ugly and neglected her,

so she and Giovanni's handsome younger brother Paolo whiled away
    the hours reading the love story of Lancelot
and Guinevere, and Francesca says, "Time and time again that reading
    led / our eyes to meet, and made our
faces pale" until "When we had read how the longed-for smile /
    was kissed by one who was so true a lover, / this one, who never

shall be parted from me, / while all his body trembled, kissed my mouth"
    and then simply "that day we read no more."
Giovanni finds out, of course—they always find out—

and the lovers are slain. You love, you die: not every time,
but there's always that risk, which is why Bruce
    Springsteen says that when you walk across the gym floor

to ask a girl to dance, what you're really doing is asking someone else
    to take your life in their hands. She could say, "Sure!
I'd love to dance with you" or "Get lost, creep!"—
        even "Get lost" is better than "Maybe" because "Maybe"
means "I don't know," whereas when you know,
    you know: in Proust's novel, Odette opens the door with a cold,

she's grumpy, her hair is in her face, her skin is blotchy, and Swann,
    who has never been drawn to her until
that moment, falls hard because she looks like a Botticelli girl from
        a damaged fresco, and the damage is part
of the attraction. "Losing love is like a window
    in your heart," says Paul Simon, who is neither a girl nor was part

of a group after he broke up with Art Garfunkel. And did he miss Art
    Garfunkel after the breakup? Sure, he did.
Paul Simon seems pretty hard-boiled, pretty thick-skinned, but I bet even
        he swiped the side of his nose with a knuckle
a time or two when he remembered how beautiful Art's
    voice was and how well they harmonized together. "The cure for

anything is salt water—tears, sweat, or the sea," says Isak Dinesen,
    and she should know. But sweat is hard
to come by, and the sea may be far away, whereas you're going to cry
        whether you want to or not and probably
sooner than you think. Thank you for helping us cry,
    girl groups. Last week in my poetry workshop, a young

woman was reading a poem about love gone wrong and burst
        into tears, and in a heartbeat, the woman next to her squeezes
her hand, and another woman two chairs away takes up
        the reading where the reader left off
in mid-sentence, the beautiful, terrible poem rolling out
        into the world, only now three women are reading it, not just one.

I BELIEVE YOU ARE DEATH

I'm on my way to Chile when I learn that the name
of its first governor is Bernardo O'Higgins,

so even though our plane is not even over Cuba yet,
not to mention Colombia, Ecuador, and Peru,

I'm in love with this skinny eel of a country, wriggling
down the Andean cordillera all the way to Tierra

del Fuego, where, according to good Sir John Mandeville,
men have no heads but mouths and eyes in their torsos.

And then there's Easter Island: how does that work?
It belongs to you, Chile, but it's 2,400 miles out

in the ocean. Chileans have droll expressions,
like *buscarle la quinta pata al gato*, which means

to look for the fifth leg of a cat, that is, to make
a simple operation overly complicated. But the best

thing about Chile is Pablo Neruda. What a poet!
Why, it's as though Keats and Frank O'Hara

collided in the air over the little town of Parral,
and Neruda falls squawling into his mother's arms,

for he has the sugary lushness of the one poet
and the conversational tone of the other,

though his tossing out of casual compliments
reminds one of Whitman as well, whose compliments

were all the more believable precisely because they
were casual and not overly elaborate and fakey.

Another droll expression is *creerse la muerte*
or believe oneself to be death, that is, cooler than

everyone else. How wonderful to love yourself
so much and not tell anyone. Actually, I love you

even more than I love myself. I believe you
to be death. I believe you to be Ambrosio

O'Higgins, father of Bernardo, himself Viceroy
of Peru and therefore someone who not only

sported a feathery plume of a name but also
a title that was nothing to sneeze at.

Only if you have read this far in this poem
will you know this. Pessimists say what

are poems good for. I say poems are good
for taking us to other countries, also

for telling you that you are beautiful.
You have to read them, though.

OLD POETS

This is South Florida, so it's steamy after the reading, even in
        January, and the two old poets walk out in front of me, the one
full of strange oaths still, jealous in honor, as sudden
        and quick in quarrel as a soldier, the other
smiling but gray and full of sleep, like a dove about to put her head

under her wing and coo, and I think, It's not going to be
        that many years before I'm an old poet myself, though
it'll be worth it if I can write the way my two old poets do
        or as Yeats did in his poem about the woman of "glad
grace" whose beauty others loved with beauty false

or true, and, before him, Shakespeare in his seven-ages
        monologue that foretells the "strange eventful history"
that is your life, her life, his, mine. What do the old
        know that we don't? At last they
understand what Kierkegaard meant when he said in *Fear*

and Trembling that "he who will not work must take
        note of what is written about the maidens of Israel,
for he gives birth to the wind, but he who is willing
        to work gives birth to his own father." No, I don't know
what it means, either! But I think Kierkegaard's saying

we should live so that our older selves will have something
        to say to the younger ones, and the younger will understand.
For example, here's old Emily Dickinson, bending beside
        the glowing bars, and she gets the feeling that she's not
alone, and that's when she realizes Young Emily is in

the room, and she's so pretty, and she has on a lovely
        dress, so Old Emily offers Young Emily a cup of tea,
and Young Emily laughs and says *I can't drink tea,*
        I don't have a body! and Old Emily says *That's so funny,*
it sounds just like one of my poems, and Young Emily

says *Oh I want to write poems* and Old Emily says
        Oh you will, and you'll have boyfriends, too, and your
lovers will sigh like furnaces, with woeful ballads
        made to their mistress's eyebrow, for you are small,
like the wren, and your hair is bold, like the chestnut

burr, and your eyes like the sherry in the glass that
        the guest leaves, and Young Emily blushes and says
Thank you! and Old Emily says *Let me finish. Because*
        you need to know your real companions will be the hills,
the sundown, and your dog Carlo. Samuel Bowles

loved me, and I could have married, but there are
        married men walking down every street in Amherst,
some having affairs, as your brother Austin will
        with Mabel Loomis Todd, herself married, and Young
Emily says *Oh dear!* and Old Emily says *But you'll do*

better. Hawthorne speaks of an allegory he wanted to
        write but never did; in it, the Heart is sunny around
its Portals, then sinister just inside, but at its core,
        a Garden, and Young Emily says *I don't want to live*
anywhere else! and Old Emily says *This is where*

you'll live, this is where you'll see your lover's hands,
  which are ravishingly beautiful, and then, a few days
later, his face, and after that, his body, which shines
    more brightly than the sun, and after that, you won't
want to open your eyes again, and after that, you'll be

a poet. My two old poets are crossing the street in front
  of me, looking left, then right, then left again before
they step off the curb, and while I could catch up easily,
    I slow a bit so I can watch them still. I know the poems
they've written so far, some by heart, and they're full

of sermons-on-the-mount, and gentle, almost as Jesus.
  What's next for them? They don't know. Neither did Monet,
Verdi, Georgia O'Keeffe, all of whom did better work
    after seventy than before. There's *a swoon God sends*
us women, says Old Emily to Young Emily, what St. Teresa

called *a radiance* and Hawthorne *an Eden,* shimmering
  like a fiery mist. No wonder she says *There's a third way,*
neither bad nor good but really good. No wonder her niece
    Martha said she pretended to lock her bedroom door once
and pocket an imaginary key, saying *Mattie, here's freedom.*

THE NEMATODE

"I'm not drunk!" my student says, though her features sag
        and her speech slurs. "The doctor's doing tests—I just
wanted you to know." She comes to class and talks about
           the assignments in her halting voice,
the other students nodding and giving her the time she needs, even

slowing their own speech so hers doesn't seem so different. A month
        later, she says, "Do you know what amyotrophic lateral
sclerosis is?" and I say, "Yes, Lou Gehrig's Disease,"
          and we cry and hug each other and go
to class, where she continues to talk, a little slower each time, until

she can't talk at all, which is when she begins to write down
        and give me everything she would have said
had she been able to say it. There's beauty in everything:
          in a man's losing his sight and saying
how lovely it is to have everyone come so close so he can recognize

them, in the woman who decides to think of her demented spouse
        as a recent addition to the family and not the man
she married years earlier, in the family that runs
          the same notice in the paper every year to tell
their dead son and brother that his place in the circle of life still brings

hope to others. We fall, but we fly first, as Jack Gilbert says
        in his great poem about Icarus. By the end
of the term, my student is dead. No one escapes
          the bitter enemy, the unbeatable opponent:
the old Greeks called it Nemesis, a word which always reminds me

of the nematode or roundworm that attacks plants in the part
       of the country where I live. My student's name
appears on the grade sheet, and I give her an A,
         even though her final paper
wasn't the strongest—what else are you going to give a dead person?

Just recently, I learn that there are two kinds of nematode,
       the root-knot variety that kills plants
and the good or predatory nematode that attacks worse
        pests, like cutworms. When I go out
into my garden at night, I look up at the sky, and sometimes I think

of what I see there, and at others I think of the scariest painting
       I know, the one in which Van Gogh
shows the heavens blazing as the little village sleeps below.
        Those stars are burning too brightly!
That fire you see can't last. Still, as it burns, it lights everything.

GNÜRSZK

When people ask you where you were and you say, "Poland!"
they always say, "Did you go to Gnürszk?" and you say,
    "Actually, I went everywhere but Gnürszk," and they say,
"Oh, you should have gone to Gnürszk—the food there
    is terrific, and it's free, and it's served by beautiful naked
people, and they give you money when you leave,"
    and you think, Why didn't we go to Gnürszk?

No, we just went to Malbork where we saw the Castle
of the Teutonic Order, the largest castle in the world
    as well as the largest brick building in Europe. And then we
strolled through Warsaw's Old Town with its alleys, squares,
    and cosy cafés. We admired the wealth of artwork,
sculptures, and silverware in Krakow's Czartoryski Museum,
    and in the countryside, we were grateful for the pleasant

landscapes, plentiful wildlife, and unique bird watching
opportunities. But we never made it to Gnürszk, where candy
    canes grow on trees and the canals are filled
with lemonade, where roasted pigs wander about with knives
    in their backs to make carving easy, cooked fish fall
from the sky, grilled ducklings fly directly into your mouth,
    the temperature is always 78 degrees, the streets are paved

with pastry, there are no clocks. If you say you went
to Germany or Italy or France, people always want to know
    if you went to Schnitzelkeit or Benzolio or Oisou-sur-Mer,
and you say no, no, you never made it to those places, either.
    But I was with the one person I wanted to be with most,
someone who loves movies and parties and books
    as much as I do, and even though it was a short trip,

we made love three times. Or was it four? Maybe it wasn't
any at all. If we'd gone to Gnürszk, we'd have had
　　wall-socket sex, the kind that shatters the bed, blows out
the windows, breaks the pipes in the bathroom
　　and floods the room below. Still, we had a good time.
Or did we? What is love, anyway? In 1982, a dentist named
　　Barney Clark became the first human recipient of an artificial

　　heart. The night before the operation, the doctors asked his wife
if she had any questions, and she said, yes—when you replace
　　his heart, will he still love me, and the doctors said yes,
of course he will, of course, of course. Maybe we'll go
　　to Gnürszk next year or the year after that. Maybe,
as the afternoon softens and turns to evening, the people
　　of Gnürszk will look out their windows and wish they were us.